Twenty in Twenty

Twenty images which helped define the 20th century

By

Allyson Lodge Hardy

Text copyright © 2020 Allyson Lodge Hardy

All rights reserved

This book is dedicated to the pioneers, the courageous, the explorers, the great leaders and those who continue to push the boundaries of what is possible.

Table of contents

Introduction 5
The Death of Queen Victoria. – end of an era...................... 7
The Wright Brothers – pioneers of flight.............................11
Shackleton's Expedition to the South Pole.........................14
Amundsen reaches the South Pole 18
The Sinking of the RMS 'Titanic'. 21
World War 1 recruitment. 27
The Discovery of the Tomb of Tutankhamun......................30
The abdication of King Edward VIII...................................35
World War 2 recruitment. 39
The birth of the NHS – envy of the world...........................41
Arrival of the package holiday 44
Ascent of Everest 49
The coronation of Queen Elizabeth II.................................54
Elvis Presley – king of rock and roll. 58
The assassination of President Kennedy 61
The Beatles – the phenomenon of 'Beatlemania'................65
The life and death of Martin Luther King. 69
Earthrise – from the Earth to the Moon 72
The invention of the computer - The Age of Technology.......75
Nelson Mandela – Fight for Freedom. 79
Acknowledgements..83
Sources:..86
By the same author:...88

Introduction

It was the early part of 2020 when I happened to notice that the date was 20.02.20. and I thought how rarely that happened.

Shortly afterwards, we were in the midst of the pandemic of COVID 19 (Coronavirus). Things were changing day by day and no-one knew what the long-term effects would be or how long it would last.

I found myself wondering what history would make of this period and then I thought about how it might compare with the happenings in the 20th century, which itself, had been a period of unprecedented change and development.

It occurred to me that I could put together a book of 20 images from areas such as technology, exploration, innovation and significant people; twenty images which helped to define the 20th century; hence the title 'Twenty in Twenty'.

When I started to research images to use, I began to realise how momentous the century had been and how many famous images there were. I selected this first group on the basis of trying to include the most recognisable photographs from across the century and covering as many areas of development and achievement as I could.

I also added a brief explanation of the story behind each image.

Of course, it soon became clear that 20 images – significant though they are – would not on their own, adequately define the century and there were at least as many more I could use. For that reason, I have already selected the twenty images which will feature in my next book, 'Twenty in Twenty More'.

I enjoyed researching this book and I learnt a great deal about the stories behind these famous photographs. I hope you enjoy them, too.

Allyson Lodge Hardy

The Death of Queen Victoria. – end of an era.

Queen Victoria (1819-1901)

With the death of Queen Victoria on January 22nd 1901, the so-called 'Victorian Era' came to an end. She was at that time, the longest reigning British monarch, having occupied the throne for 63 years. She was the last British monarch of the House of Hanover and the first to live in Buckingham Palace.

Princess Alexandrina Victoria of Kent (1819-1901) was born at Kensington Palace in London, the daughter of Prince Edward, Duke of Kent and Strathearn and his wife, Princess Victoria of Saxe-Coburg Saalfield.

Victoria's father, the Duke and his father, King George III, died in 1820 and subsequently, her father's three older brothers died without any surviving legitimate children. This left Victoria as the heir to the throne at the age of 18.

In 1840, Victoria married her cousin, Prince Albert of Saxe-Coburg and Gotha and they had nine children: Victoria (b 1840), Albert Edward (b 1841), Alice (b 1843), Alfred (b 1844), Helena (b 1846), Louise (b 1848), Arthur (b 1850), Leopold (b 1853), Beatrice (b 1857).

Victoria didn't like children – especially babies – and she struggled to have any kind of positive relationship with her own. It seems she was a very controlling and demanding parent who would openly criticise her children to each other and to others throughout their lives. The Queen's desire to control the lives of her nine children continued even when they were adults.

Victoria often said that her own childhood was lonely and unhappy and that she felt unloved by her mother, yet when her mother died in 1820, Victoria found little notes and letters written to her during her childhood by the Duchess, which seemed to show that she was extremely fond of her daughter.

In 1845, Victoria and Albert bought the private estate of Osborne House on the Isle of Wight and used it as a retreat from public life and in 1852, they purchased Balmoral in Scotland. Prince Albert said the scenery reminded him of his homeland.

When Prince Albert died in 1861 – possibly of typhoid fever - Victoria was devastated. She had relied on him completely – even to the most mundane of daily tasks- and without him she was lost. During her many pregnancies and convalescences, Albert had taken on most of the duties of State.

Victoria went into a protracted period of deep mourning from which she never fully emerged, wearing black for the rest of her life. She became a virtual recluse for the first couple of years after Albert's death.

Victoria had always needed a strong male figure to lean on. The first was her Prime Minister, Lord Melbourne. They developed a close friendship and she relied on him for advice and support. He was the father figure she had never had. The second was Prince Albert, who filled the role throughout their marriage.

A Highland servant named John Brown – whom she met at Balmoral - became Victoria's friend and confidante and there were rumours of an affair. She was even given the nickname 'Mrs Brown', though there has never been any evidence that their relationship was anything other than that of close friends. John Brown was devoted to Victoria and she trusted him completely. Her children did not approve.

In the same way that Victoria had 'favourites' amongst her children, she also had Prime Ministers with whom she was on good terms. Apart from Lord Melbourne, Benjamin

Disraeli was a particular favourite. He knew how to flatter Victoria and when he died, she was genuinely grief-stricken. On the other hand, she had little time for Robert Peel (founder of the modern police force) and no time at all for his successor, Gladstone.

Bertie, the heir to the throne was a notorious womaniser and this behaviour continued even after Victoria had arranged his marriage to the beautiful and accomplished Princess May of Teck. Victoria wrote to one of her daughters saying that she hoped she would outlive her son as he would make a most unsuitable king.

Victoria and at least two of her daughters – Alice and Beatrice - were carriers of the haemophilia gene and her youngest son Leopold, suffered from the disease. Since most of Victoria and Albert's children had been married to various dukes and princes and princesses across Europe, Victoria inadvertently caused the spread of haemophilia throughout many of the royal families of Europe.

Legend has it that Queen Victoria coined the phrase "We are not amused" and certainly, photographs of her laughing or smiling are rare. There is no evidence that she ever said this and indeed, she always denied it. Her friends and many of her courtiers asserted that she had a good sense of humour and laughed loudly and often.

Queen Victoria, Empress of India died on January 22nd 1901 at Osborne House and is buried next to her beloved Albert in the royal burial site at Frogmore, Windsor

The Wright Brothers – pioneers of flight.

Orville and Wilbur Wright

19.08.1871 – 30.01.48 and 16.04.1867 – 30.05.1912

Brothers Orville and Wilbur Wright were born to Milton and Susan Koener Wright of Dayton, Ohio. The couple met whilst he was training for the Ministry and she was at college.

Milton was an ordained minister who became a bishop in 1877 and the family moved often but eventually settled back in Dayton in 1884.

The parents placed a great deal of emphasis on education, not just being taught but finding out for themselves, feeding their curiosity and encouraging their family to be independent thinkers. This instilled self-confidence, belief in themselves, perseverance in adversity and a determination to succeed.

Orville convinced Wilbur to join him in setting up a printing business. They produced three newspapers, including one for the African- American community. The brothers designed and built high-quality printing presses, which they sold to other printers. These were some of their early experiments in design and engineering.

In 1892, the brothers opened a shop making, repairing and selling bicycles.

Profits from the bicycle shop and printing business funded their early experiments in aeronautics between 1899 and 1905. They had developed this interest when they were living in Iowa (1876-1881) and their father bought them a toy helicopter.

In 1900, the brothers introduced themselves to Octave Chanute, a civil engineer and an authority on aviation, who helped and advised them and the three became firm friends.

Orville and Wilbur realised that in order to fly, a plane needed three things; wings to generate lift, a propulsion system to move it forward through the air and a method of controlling the plane when it was in the air. They wanted to place complete control of their flying machine in the hands of the operator.

Early experiments with a small bi-plane in 1899 demonstrated that they could make it dive, rise and bank to the left and right, so they began work on a full-scale glider.

The conditions in Dayton were unsuitable for their experiments as it was flat and there was very little wind, so the brothers moved to Kitty Hawk, North Carolina where there was soft sand to land on, tall dunes to glide from and stronger average winds.

Early tests in October 1900 were disappointing; the aircraft had less lift than expected so they increased the area of the wings. There was some improvement but the plane did not perform as well as expected. The brothers kept experimenting throughout 1901 and 1902.

On the morning of December 17th 1903, Orville made the first successful flight, achieving a distance of 120 feet (36 metres) in 12 seconds, then Wilbur flew 175 feet (53 metres) in 10 seconds. Orville had a second attempt and managed 200 feet (60 metres) in 15 seconds. Wilbur then had two more attempts and flew a total of 852 feet (260 metres) in 59 seconds.

The brothers continued to develop and improve their design and by October 1905, they had perfected their machine to enable it to remain airborne for up to 29 minutes and perform various manoeuvres.

They paved the way for today's aeronautics industry.

Shackleton's Expedition to the South Pole.

HMS 'Endurance'
Photographed by expedition photographer, Frank Hurley.

Ernest Henry Shackleton was born in County Kildare, Ireland on February 15th 1874.

His first experience of the Polar regions was as Third Officer on Captain Scott's 'Discovery' expedition (1901-1904) but it seems that Scott and Shackleton didn't get on too well.

When Shackleton became ill on the expedition, he was sent home early on health grounds but not before he, Scott and their comrade Edward Wilson (who would later sail with Scott's ill-fated 'Terra Nova' expedition) had successfully reached 82 degrees south, a point further south than anyone had reached before

Shackleton was on the 'Nimrod' expedition in 1907, which brought him to 88 degrees south, within two degrees of the South Pole.

In 1912, Shackleton began planning another expedition to the South Pole, this time with the aim of crossing Antarctica from the Weddell Sea to the Ross Sea. He announced his plans in 1914 and began raising the funds.

Having carefully selected what he felt to be the best men to serve as crew on this voyage, there was a concern that it would be delayed or even cancelled because of the outbreak of World War 1 in 1914. However, Shackleton received a telegram from Winston Churchill, who was then First Lord of the Admiralty. The telegram contained only one word "Proceed" so 'Endurance' left British waters on August 8th.

Shackleton left at the end of September and met up with his crew and his ship in Buenos Aires and on December 5th, they departed the island of South Georgia for the Weddell Sea.

It was unfortunate for the expedition that the ice formed early that year and was exceptionally thick. On January 15th, the ship became stuck in the ice and had to drift along with it, hoping that it would disintegrate but by August 15th, they were forced to abandon the 'Endurance' to its fate. They camped on the ice. They managed to salvage three open boats, some small items of equipment and whatever supplies they could carry.

It was at this time that Frank Hurley took some memorable images of the ship.

The ship broke up in October and finally sank in November.

The crew sailed their small boats through heavy seas to Elephant Island, some 346 miles (557 km) from where 'Endurance' sank. It took them 5 days and when they finally reached this inhospitable piece of rock, it was the first time they had stood on solid ground for 497 days.

Shackleton decided that the only option was to take one of the boats and sail for South Georgia -720 nautical miles away - and find rescue. It was unlikely that they would ever be found if they stayed on Elephant Island; no-one knew where they were to start looking for them.

Five men accompanied Shackleton on this long and dangerous voyage – McNish, Crean, Worsley, Vincent and McCarthy - and they all knew they might never arrive at South Georgia, let alone return with a rescue party.

McNish – the ship's carpenter - strengthened the 'James Caird' and added a makeshift deck and Shackleton took only four weeks- worth of supplies, realising that if they hadn't reached land and help in four weeks, they wouldn't make it at all.

They endured 15 days rough sailing on high seas then were prevented from landing due to hurricane-force winds: they had to land on the uninhabited part of the island, the opposite side from where they needed to be. From there, they had to walk for 36 hours to reach the whaling station. They finally arrived on May 20th.

A rescue party was formed but bad weather delayed them until finally, on August 30th 1916, the rescue party arrived at Elephant Island. All 22 men were alive and well and in remarkably good spirits, especially considering they had been marooned there for 4 ½ months.

When he returned home, Shackleton toured the lecture circuit until 1920 but tired of that and began planning another voyage to the Antarctic in 1921. Several of the former 'Endurance' crew signed on with him.

On reaching Rio de Janeiro, Shackleton had a suspected minor heart attack but refused treatment or further investigation. He ordered the ship to sail south and the following day – January 5th 1922 – he died. His wife requested that he be buried on South Georgia.

In an address to the British Science Association in 1956, geologist and Antarctic explorer Sir Raymond Priestley, paid tribute to three men whose names will be forever linked with Antarctic exploration: Scott, Amundsen and Shackleton. "Scott for scientific method, Amundsen for speed and efficiency but when disaster strikes and all hope is gone, get down on your knees and pray for Shackleton".

Amundsen reaches the South Pole

Roald Amundsen and his team planting the Norwegian flag at the South Pole. 1911.

Roald Amundsen was born in Borge, Norway on 16th July 1872, the fourth son of Jens Amundsen and Hanna Stahlqvist.

The family members were shipowners and sea captains but Roald's mother wanted him to become a doctor, so he went to university to study medicine.

Roald's mother died when he was 21 so he left university and went to sea.

When he was 15, Amundsen had read the accounts by explorer Sir John Franklin, of his Arctic expeditions and was captivated. Later, he would write "I read them with a fervid fascination which has shaped the whole course of my life." Amundsen himself spoke of the lure of exploring a territory where no human had previously set foot.

After first joining a Belgian Antarctic expedition as first mate then leading an expedition to navigate the North West Passage, Amundsen turned his attention to planning an Arctic expedition. He borrowed a ship from Nansen which was called the 'Fram' and set about raising funds through donations and sponsorship.

In 1909, Amundsen learned that two American explorers each claimed to have reached the North Pole, so he focused on planning an expedition to the South Pole instead. He kept the destination secret, even from his own crew until they left Madeira, their final port of call.

They set out in June 1910.

A British expedition under Capt. R F Scott was also heading south, in the belief that Amundsen was heading north but as he started his journey, Amundsen sent Scott a telegram which simply read "Am heading south".

Amundsen and his team set up their base in the Bay of Whales on the Great Ice Barrier and named it 'Fromheim', after the ship.

Following months of preparation, the team finally set off in search of the Pole in October 1911.

En route, they discovered the Axel Heiberg Glacier, which provided a route for the team to reach the polar plateau. Amundsen named the glacier after a wealthy businessman who had contributed to several Norwegian polar expeditions.

The team used sled dogs and skis to traverse the region, which led to a relatively speedy journey to the South Pole and they arrived on December 14th. Two days later, the Norwegian flag was raised at the site.

This was a tremendous achievement and widely celebrated, although it was slightly tempered when news of Scott's 'heroic failure' reached the rest of the world. Amundsen had arrived at the South Pole five weeks before Scott and his team, who all died on the return journey.

Since 1956 there has been a permanent scientific research station at the South Pole. Named the Amundsen-Scott Station and built in 1956 for the Federal Government of the United States, the base has been continuously occupied since then.

In 1957, the Scott Base was constructed. Named in honour of Capt. R F Scott, this New Zealand Antarctic Research Facility is located near Mount Erebus.

The Sinking of the RMS 'Titanic'.

The pride of the White Star Line – RMS 'Titanic'

RMS 'Titanic' was built at the Harland and Wolff shipyard in Belfast and was one of a trio of luxury liners of the Olympic class, built to rival their competitor Cunard's 'Lusitania' and 'Mauretania'. The other two ships in the new fleet were the 'Britannic' and the 'Olympic'.

Bruce Ismay – Chairman and CEO of the White Star Line – oversaw the design of the ship, during which he had the number of lifeboats reduced from 48 to 16. This wasn't just about money, simply that at that time, the British Board of Trade's outdated regulations regarding lifeboats, were based on a ship's tonnage, not the number of passengers and had failed to keep up with the rapid increase in larger passenger-carrying vessels. At the time therefore, Ismay's decision was perhaps unwise but not unreasonable.

The 'Titanic' was the most luxurious ship afloat and had every modern convenience, such as a heated swimming pool (for first class passengers only), a gymnasium and the new Marconi radio system and she was said to be 'unsinkable'.

She also had the White Star Line's most famous and experienced Captain on its maiden voyage, Edward Smith. Smith was known as the 'Millionaires' Captain' and this was to be his final voyage before retiring.

The ship was launched on May 31st 1911.

When she set out across the Atlantic on her maiden voyage, the 'Titanic' was carrying 2240 passengers and crew and whilst she was known to be carrying many wealthy first-class passengers – including John Jacob Astor (who would later refuse his place in lifeboat number four), Benjamin Guggenheim and the owner of Macy's, Isidor Strauss and his wife, Ida – many of those on board were third class passengers, around 700 of them.

The shipping lines made most of their profits from third class passengers, much in the way that airlines make their profits from economy class passengers rather than first class today.

A first- class ticket for a simple berth cost $150 (around $1700 today), the Parlour Suites each cost $4350 (around $50,000 today). A second- class ticket was $60 ($700 today) and third -class passengers paid between $15 and $40 (equivalent to $170 to $460).

Whilst there are many myths and even a few conspiracy theories about the sinking of the 'Titanic', there were certainly a number of unfortunate coincidences which contributed to the ship's ultimate fate.

Firstly, there were a number of watertight bulkheads installed in the ship and had they reached up to the deck, the ship would have been at little risk of flooding but they only reached part of the way. This meant that if one area flooded, instead of being able to seal it off, there was nothing to prevent the water running over the top of one bulkhead into the next one.

Secondly, a small but significant fire had occurred in one of the coal bunkers before the voyage started and whilst it was brought under control, it had been intense and had burned for a considerable time, thus warping the steel plates. This was to be significant once the ship started to take on water.

Thirdly, the bow of the ship had been reinforced to take the impact should she hit an iceberg or another ship, so had the 'Titanic' hit the iceberg head on, she would probably have survived. As it was, the lookouts did not spot the iceberg until it was too late and the instinct of the officer on watch was to steer away from the iceberg, leaving it to slice open the metal plates under the waterline.

It was also an exceptionally calm night; had the sea not been as calm, the lookouts would have seen waves breaking against the iceberg and been able to call out a warning much earlier.

For some reason, Captain Smith had cancelled the scheduled lifeboat drill so the crew was untried and untrained on manning and releasing the lifeboats.

There had been more icebergs than usual sighted in the shipping lanes that April and they had moved further south than was normal. Captain Smith had been receiving iceberg warnings from other ships all that day and as a precaution, he had ordered that the ship take a route further south in order to avoid any icebergs.

Unwittingly, he put the ship on a collision course with the enormous iceberg, which would be the instrument that would send her two and a half miles to the bottom of the Atlantic Ocean in around two and a half hours and take 1500 souls with her.

The wireless operators -who worked for Marconi, not for the White Star Line – made their money by sending 'ship to shore' messages from passengers but they also received messages from other ships. If the message was for the captain, it would be sent with an MSG (Master Service Gram) prefix.

On the night of the disaster, a message was sent to the 'Titanic' from another ship, warning of heavy ice in the area and advising that she had stopped for the night. This message did not come with the customary MSG prefix so was not taken to the captain straight away.

Furthermore, when the operators came within range of the Cape Race receiver, they had a great many passenger messages to send out, so when the 'Californian' sent a message warning about icebergs in the vicinity, she was so close that the radio operator on the 'Titanic' was nearly deafened! He sent back a message telling the operator on the 'Californian' to get off the radio as he was transmitting to Cape Race. The radio operator on the 'Californian' switched off his radio and went to bed for the night.

The 'Californian' was the only ship close enough to have saved everyone on board the 'Titanic' but with her radio switched off, she was deaf to the stricken ship's increasingly urgent calls for help.

In the past, the call for immediate assistance was given as 'CQZ' but the Titanic's radio operator also gave the new call sign, 'SOS'. Although another ship – the 'Carpathia' - was in radio range and immediately turned and headed for the 'Titanic', it became obvious that she would not reach the rapidly sinking ship in time.

When the news broke, the reaction was one of horror and disbelief. How could this have happened to an 'unsinkable' ship?

The British Board of Trade held an inquiry into a tragedy which was as least in part, of its own making but clearly it was not found to have been culpable. It also stated that the cause of death of the passengers was due to drowning but this was not necessarily the case. It was realised many years later that most of the victims would probably have died as a result of hypothermia, not drowning.

In 1985, the wreck of the 'Titanic' was found by Dr Robert Ballard and his team from Woods Hole Oceanographic Institution and it was shown that the ship had broken up before hitting the ocean floor.

Later, RMS 'Titanic' Inc – legal custodian of the wreck – carried out extensive surveys of the site, to try and find out how and why the great ship sank. Their work produced 160 hours of video footage, 37 terabytes of data and a 3D model from millions of data points obtained by scanning the ocean floor.

Aside from mapping the area and identifying its size and boundaries, the project also proved definitively that the iceberg had not torn a 300 foot (91 metre) gash in the side of the vessel, as many had believed and indeed, as had been stated in the report of the British Board of Trade. The damage is confined to an area of perhaps 30 feet (10 metres), which would allow water to gush in at 370 gallons a second. This would mean that the estimated time of two and a half hours that it took the ship to sink, would be correct.

Of the 2240 souls who set sail on that magnificent ship, there were only 705 survivors and only 340 bodies were ever recovered. Three cemeteries in Halifax, Nova Scotia have areas reserved for victims of the 'Titanic'.

World War 1 recruitment.

World War 1 recruitment poster

When this image was produced in 1914, it was the first time since the Napoleonic Wars that a recruitment poster had been used to encourage men to join the army. For a hundred years, the British Army had been 'voluntary'.

Field Martial Horatio Herbert Kitchener (1st Lord Kitchener, 1850-1916) was born in County Kerry, Ireland. He made his name in the Battle of Andurman (1898), wresting back control of the Sudan and subsequently in the Second Boer War, where he was Chief of Staff (1900-1902) before becoming Commander-in-Chief of the Army in India (1902-1909).

In August 1914, Prime Minister Herbert Henry Asquith (1852-1928) appointed Lord Kitchener as Secretary of State for War. He was the first serving soldier to hold the post.

Kitchener was tasked with recruiting a large army to help the country in its fight against Germany.

John Seely (1st Baron Mottistone) was the Secretary of State for War and had awarded a contract to publishers Hedley le Bas and its advertising agency, Caxton's, to run adverts in the leading newspapers to assist with recruitment into the military.

Alfred Leete was one of Caxton's illustrators and he created the famous poster for the 5th September edition of the London Opinion newspaper. Kitchener's commanding appearance – he was 6 ft 2 inches tall and well-built – his military record and his recent appointment as Secretary of State for War, made him the perfect subject. Certainly. the poster seemed to do its job; September 1914 saw the largest number of recruits volunteering to enlist.

Lord Kitchener was killed in action in 1916 when his ship was blown up by a German mine.

His image lives on through this famous poster, which has become one of the most iconic images of World War 1.

The Discovery of the Tomb of Tutankhamun

The golden mask of Tutankhamun.

The tomb of Tutankhamun was one of the greatest archaeological discoveries ever made. It was the first truly scientific excavation carried out on a tomb and provided a blueprint for modern archaeology, where the preservation of artifacts and the search for information is the greater treasure.

George Edward Stanhope Molyneaux Herbert, Lord Porchester, 5th Earl of Carnarvon was born on 26th June 1866 at the family seat of Highclere Castle in Berkshire. He succeeded his father as Earl in 1890.

In 1895, he married Almina Wombwell of the wealthy Rothschild family and received a £500,000 marriage settlement, which not only helped to pay off some of the Earl's debts but also made him a very wealthy man. He became well known as a racehorse owner and also indulged his passion for fast cars.

It was a car crash in 1901 which led to the Earl's presence in Egypt.

His injuries had left him with a permanent weakness and his doctors advised that the Egyptian climate might be beneficial, so the Earl and his wife began spending winters in Egypt and became enthusiastic amateur Egyptologists, buying antiquities for their personal collection.

Carnarvon had the money to indulge his hobby but not the knowledge and when he decided to sponsor a dig at Deir el-Bahari, Gaston Maspero of the Egyptian Antiquities Department, recommended Howard Carter.

Carter was born into a family of nine children in Kensington, London on 9th May 1874 but spent much of his childhood in Swaffam, Norfolk. Carter's father was a gifted artist, a gift he passed on to his son. They lived close to Didlington Hall, which had a collection of Egyptian artifacts. Lady Amherst was impressed by Carter's artistic ability and arranged for the Egypt Exploration Fund to send Carter to Egypt when he was only 17.

Carter's main role was to copy the inscriptions in tombs and temples and for a time he served under the father of Egyptology, Sir William Matthew Flinders Petrie. It was whilst working for Petrie that Carter learnt many of the skills of excavation which would serve him well in later years.

Coincidentally, his first job with Petrie was copying inscriptions at Amarna, the city where Tutankhamun was born.

Fate would bring Carter and Carnarvon together and they would go on to make one of the greatest discoveries of all time.

Funded by Carnarvon, Carter excavated at various sites and they were rewarded only with a few trinkets and a mummified cat but Carter always had his eye on a greater prize, the Valley of the Kings, where he knew that the greatest prize of all – the tomb of Tutankhamun – was to be found.

Theodore Davis – a wealthy but eccentric American lawyer – had the concession to dig in the Kings' Valley but in 1914 he declared publicly that "The Valley of the Kings is now exhausted" and he relinquished his concession, which was eagerly taken up by Carnarvon.

Carter spent six years – apart from a brief hiatus during the First World War -digging systematically in the valley and found nothing. With so little progress, Carnarvon became disenchanted and said he couldn't continue to fund the excavations but Carter begged for one more season, which he even offered to fund himself.

Carnarvon relented and agreed to Carter's request.

The season started on November 1st 1922 and progress was remarkably swift. On November 4th, Hussein Abdul-Rassoul - the water boy and most junior member of the team – discovered what turned out to be the first step of a flight of stone steps leading to the door of a tomb. By the end of the month, the corridor had been cleared of rubble, the team gained access to the antechamber and then to the treasury and burial chamber.

The reason that the tomb had remained undiscovered – apart from two attempts at robbery in ancient times (the robbers were discovered and the priests repaired the damaged caused during the breach) – was that the entrance was covered with debris created during the construction of the later tomb of Ramesses VI.

Carnarvon had made a deal with The Times newspaper, giving them exclusive rights to the story of the discovery, which angered the other papers as they lost many copies to The Times. To try and reclaim some of the story, two journalists came up with the story of the curse and even in the 21st century, there are people who still believe it.

Some of the most illustrious learning establishments in the world offered their finest experts to assist Carter and he took up the offers.

Every item was numbered and catalogued with one of Carter's drawings to accompany the description, then the great Harry Burton photographed each item *in situ* then removed and photographed it on its own against a neutral background.

The first object was removed from the tomb on December 27th 1922 and it took ten years to clear the tomb.

Many preservation techniques had to be invented on the spot and all items had to be conserved and stabilised before being carefully packed and sent to Cairo, where they can still be seen today.

It is a tribute to all those involved that of the more than 10,000 objects removed from the tomb, less than half a percent were lost or damaged.

Sadly, Lord Carnarvon would not live to see the end result of his project. He was bitten by a mosquito and cut the bite mark when he was shaving. Due to his already weak constitution, septicaemia set in and he developed pneumonia. He died on 5th April 1923 and is buried on Beacon Hill, overlooking Highclere castle.

The abdication of King Edward VIII

Wallis Simpson formerly (Wallis Spencer nee Wallis Warfield) and Edward, Prince of Wales in 1934.

Edward Albert Christian George Andrew Patrick David. Prince of Wales and heir apparent to King George V, was born in 1894. He was the eldest of the six children born to King George V and Queen Mary.

The King was stern and strict with his offspring and this showed itself in adulthood in different ways. Edward – known as David to his family and close friends – enjoyed rebelling against the staid, old-fashioned traditions (as he saw them) embodied by the King.

Prince Edward had several married mistresses and would spend time with them at the expense of his royal duties. He was known for not being punctual, for his outlandish dress, for his habit of getting involved in politics and for his love of attending parties and nightclubs with his 'cocktail set'.

In 1931, he was at a house party at the home of one of his mistresses – Lady Thelma (pronounced 'Telma') Furness – when he was introduced to Wallis Simpson and her husband Ernest. The Prince was immediately attracted to her sharp wit, lack of deference and her American straight-talking.

Shortly after, Thelma was going to visit her relatives in America and asked Wallis to "Look after the little man". Wallis took Thelma's request a little too literally and by the time Thelma returned, she had been frozen out and Wallis had become the Prince's new 'favourite'.

In the early days of the relationship, Ernest Simpson appears to have been compliant and to have enjoyed the perks of being a member of the Prince's 'inner circle' but soon, he became tired of having to share his wife. Ernest was seen less and less as the relationship between Wallis and Edward grew and in turn, Edward was becoming more obsessed with his mistress, taking her on holidays, buying her furs and expensive jewellery and being seen with her at theatres and parties.

When King George heard that his eldest son had given an unknown woman £100,000 of jewels (the equivalent of around £7 million today) he suspected his son was being blackmailed and through the Prime Minister, he asked Scotland Yard to provide surveillance on this woman.

The King despaired and was heard to say that when he was dead, "the boy will ruin himself within a year". He was worried about the stability of the monarchy and with good reason, as later events would show.

Edward believed that he could marry Wallis and make her his Queen in spite of the fact that she was a commoner, an American but more importantly, she had been twice divorced and had two husbands living.

Wallis loved the life that Edward had introduced her to but did not believe the relationship would last so she made the most of it while she could. It also became clear much later that she did not love Edward. Letters were found which Wallis had written to Ernest, saying how much she missed him and worried about him and acknowledging what a happy and contented life they had had together.

Wallis had tried to end the relationship with Edward several times but he would not agree, even going so far as to threaten to kill himself if she left him.

Letters from Ernest to his mother also proved that he had colluded in the divorce by allowing himself to be caught in a hotel room with another woman, thus giving Wallis grounds to divorce him so her relationship with Edward would not be dragged through the divorce courts.

The Prime Minister, Stanley Baldwin and his Government would not accept the idea of making a divorced woman Queen and as the King was head of the Church of England, it was difficult to see how this could be managed. A Morganatic Marriage was suggested (this is where a commoner marries a royal but does not share royal rank) but this required special legislation which the Government would not approve.

Finally, even Edward had to concede that he could not be king with Wallis at his side so he decided to abdicate the throne in favour of his brother, Albert (known as Bertie), who took the name King George VI at his coronation.

Edward and Wallis moved to France, where they married on June 3rd 1937.

Wallis was considered to be the villain and has been vilified for 'stealing' the king from his country and people.

What was not known at the time was that Wallis and Edward were both being spied on by MI5 on the instruction of King George V and later, on the orders of King George VI.

Wallis and Edward lived in Paris until his death from throat cancer in 1972. Wallis died in 1986 at the age of almost 90. They are buried together in the Royal Burial Ground at Frogmore near Windsor.

(Recently, documents in the British Archives have been declassified and they show that during the covert operation to spy on Wallis and Edward, there were suspicions that they could be 5th Column. They had visited Nazi Germany, had tea with Hitler and visited Goebbels. Later, it transpired that Edward had made it known that if the Labour Party in England was in a position to offer it, he was prepared to become President of the English Republic and remove his brother from the throne).

World War 2 recruitment.

World War 2 recruitment poster.

This WW2 recruitment poster entitled 'Together' and designed to depict 'strength in unity', was designed by William Little and produced by the Ministry of Information It was passed for publication in August 1941.

The poster shows soldiers, sailors and airmen marching with the Union Flag but it was intended to represent the British and Commonwealth nations and others. In total, 15 million men and women from the Commonwealth, colonies and Imperial Indian forces fought and served alongside Britain and her allies.

This was very much a war with the message 'we're all in this together' and 'we can all do our part'. Posters and Public Information films exhorted everyone to grow their own food, recycle clothes, 'make do and mend', not to waste food and to share their air raid shelters. The language was about fortitude, courage, resolution, determination and resilience.

Everyone was warned about the dangers of talking recklessly about names and numbers of ships and the whereabouts of troops because anyone could be a spy. There is a particularly graphic poster showing a drowning man at sea with the caption 'Somebody Talked'.

Women were positively encouraged to work in munitions factories or the Land Army, to drive buses or fire trucks, act as Air Raid Wardens or train as mechanics.

The armed services personnel and civilians who served are remembered and acknowledged every November in the Remembrance Day Parade in London. Representatives of the Commonwealth, colonies and overseas territories are always represented.

The birth of the NHS – envy of the world.

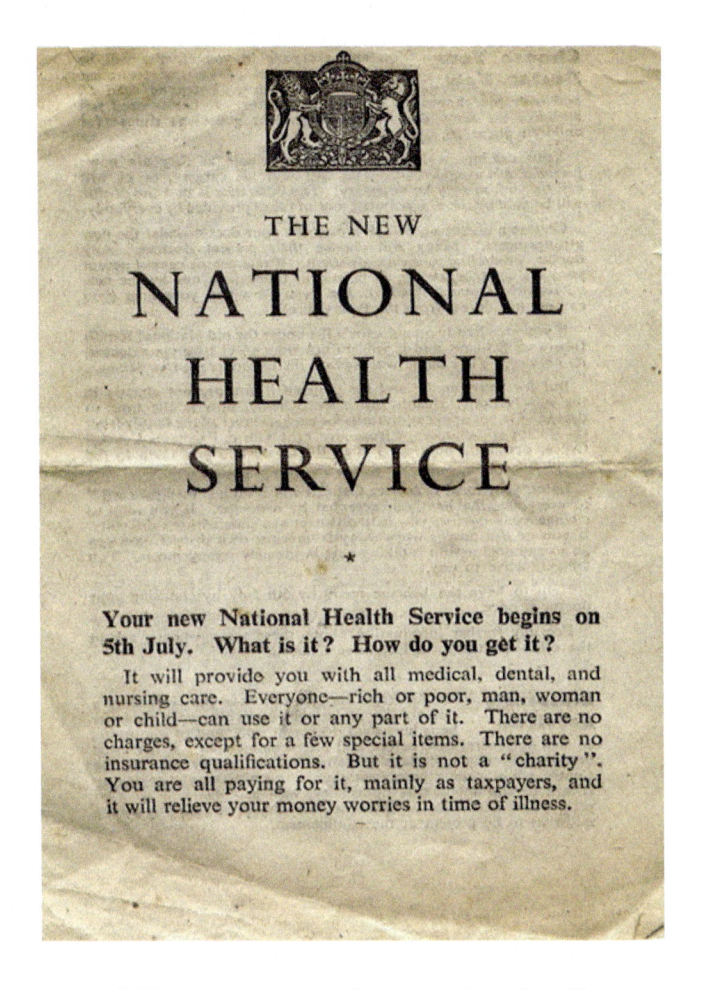

Public Service Information leaflet.

Prior to the creation of the NHS, patients faced unequal treatment and often could not afford such medication as was available then. They had to pay for treatment and there was a system of voluntary aided hospitals.

The NHS Act was brought before Parliament in 1946 as part of a social welfare policy for those in need. The main principle was to provide a comprehensive service funded through taxation, which was available to everyone who needed it and free at the point of delivery.

On July 5th 1948, the NHS took control of 480,000 hospital beds in England and Wales. Around 5,000 consultants and 125,000 nurses – their training and educational requirements increased – were available to care for hospital patients. At that time there was a tremendous shortage of nurses (around 48,000), inadequate and insufficient equipment and hospitals which were old, in disrepair and not fit for purpose.

Aneurine Bevan, writing in 'The Lancet' in 1948 stated "My job is to give you all the facilities, resources and help I can and then leave you alone - as professional men and women – to use your skills and judgement without hindrance".

In its first year, the NHS cost £248 million to run, almost £148 million more than anticipated. In 1952, there was a charge of 1 shilling (5p) for prescriptions and £1 for basic dental treatment.

The first baby born under the NHS system was Aneira Thomas, born at a minute after midnight on July 5th 1948 at a hospital in Wales.

1958 saw the first mass vaccination programme, with all those aged 15 and over being vaccinated against polio and diphtheria.

In 1961, the contraceptive pill became available to married women and in 1967, this was extended to include single women.

The first full hip replacement was carried out in 1967 by Professor Sir John Charnley and in 1968 – following on from the world's first successful heart transplant carried out by Christian Barnard - the first UK heart transplant was carried out by a team of 18 doctors and nurses, working under Sir

Terence English. The operation took place at Papworth Hospital in Cambridgeshire and the patient lived for another five years.

The introduction of new technology helped to speed up diagnosis and one of the earliest pieces of new equipment was the CT (Computerised Tomography) Scanner, now considered essential. It was used for the first time in 1972.

In 1978, there was another major breakthrough when the first so-called 'test tube' baby Louise Brown, was born.

In 1988, the MMR vaccine was introduced in the UK to replace separate vaccines for Measles, Mumps and Rubella; three infectious childhood diseases which could have serious consequences for adults, as well as many children.

The NHS celebrated its 50th birthday in 1998 and whilst it has undergone – and continues to undergo – many changes and challenges, it remains true to its original mission:

To meet the needs of everyone
To be free at the point of delivery
To be based on clinical need, not ability to pay.

Arrival of the package holiday

The bureaucracy of travel

Thomas Cook can legitimately claim to be the father of the modern package holiday.

Born in Melbourne, Derbyshire in 1802, he was brought up as a Baptist and became a village evangelist. After moving to Market Harborough, Leicestershire in 1882, he took the Temperance Pledge on January 1st 1833.

This led to his first organised tour, when in 1841, he took a party of temperance campaigners from Leicester to a rally in Loughborough. Five hundred people paid one shilling each for the return journey by rail. This was followed by an excursion to Liverpool and Wales in 1845.

In 1846, Cook took 350 people from Leicestershire on a tour of Scotland and in 1851, he made the arrangements for 150,000 people to travel to the Great Exhibition in London.

Thomas Cook's organised tours paved the way for bus and rail companies to offer short breaks to all parts of the UK and these are still popular today.

Thomas Cook's first tour abroad took place in 1855 when he arranged for two groups to travel to Belgium and Germany, ending up in France. Soon after – and even to this day – the name of Thomas Cook became synonymous with tours of Egypt and the Holy Land.

In the 1800's the only way of transporting people from one country to another was by sea and in 1819, the SS 'Savannah' became the first dual steamer/sailing ship to cross the Atlantic carrying passengers. Most of the journey had to be carried out under sail due to the weather conditions and the journey took 27 ½ days.

This paved the way for more regular Trans-Atlantic passenger services and ships became larger, faster and more luxurious. They included the 'Lusitania' and the 'Mauretania' – both of which belong to the Cunard line – and of course the White Star Line's ill-fated 'Titanic'. For her time, the RMS 'Titanic' was the most modern and most luxurious ship afloat.

The popularity of the great liners declined when Trans-Atlantic flights became available but in the 1970's, there was a resurgence in interest, led by the possibility of passengers being able to visit several countries during a single holiday and the new cruise industry was born. Mediterranean and Caribbean cruises became available as well as the Norwegian Fjords, the Baltic and the Red Sea.

The first cross-Channel passenger-carrying ferry was the English-built paddle-steamer 'Rob Roy', which travelled to France in 1821. Soon there were regular cross-Channel ferry links between ports such as Dover and Calais, Folkestone and Boulogne and Newhaven and Dieppe, managed by a small number of companies including P&O, Brittany Ferries and Townsend Thoresen.

As well as reliable transport, a key requirement for travellers is somewhere comfortable to stay and two pioneers of luxury hotels were born in the 1800's. Cesar Ritz ('King of Hoteliers and Hotelier to Kings') was born in 1850 and opened his first luxury hotel in Paris in 1898. Conrad Hilton was born in 1887. The first Hilton hotel was opened in Texas in 1925.

As international travel began to increase, there came the problem of travellers having to carry money in various denominations, depending on which countries they were travelling to. To combat this problem, Thomas Cook introduced the 'circular note' in 1874. This was the forerunner of the travellers' cheque and could be exchanged for meals and accommodation at selected hotels.

By the 1980's, the increased use of credit cards, the arrival of the Euro and the growth of the 'all inclusive' holiday, meant that the use of travellers' cheques began to decline.

In the early 1900's, the Wright Brothers pioneered a new form of transport with their first sustained flight being completed in 1903. It was followed in 1927 by Charles Lindbergh's solo Trans-Atlantic flight from New York to Paris. This changed the public perception about air travel and it is now the mainstay of the modern package holiday.

Travelling abroad was still rare in the first half of the 20th century and only for the wealthy. For the rest of the population, there were no paid holidays until 1938, when the 'Holiday With Pay' Act came into force.

In 1906, J Fletcher Dodd opened a holiday camp with hut-based accommodation and this led to the development of holiday camps by Billy Butlin, who opened his first camp in Skegness in 1936. Harry Warner (founder of the Warner Leisure Group), opened his first camp at Hayling Island in Hampshire in 1931. This was followed by the first Pontin's holiday camp which opened at Bream in Somerset in 1946.

Finally, families could holiday together and food, accommodation and entertainment were all part of the package. They can be considered the forerunner of the modern 'all-inclusive' holiday.

For those wishing to travel further afield, the advent of charter flights in the 1950's brought this a step closer.

The first charter flight from the UK took place in 1950 and was from London's Gatwick Airport to the island of Corsica. It was run by the Horizon company.

The first modern package holiday took place in 1952 and the destination was Palma, Spain. Spain was the first mass tourist destination and the average cost of a two-week package holiday in the 1950's was £35 per person. It was the equivalent about 1/5 of the average annual salary but once there, food and drink were cheap.

In the 1970's, package holidays became more affordable and their popularity increased. In the 1980's, 'specialist' holidays began to develop. They included ski-ing trips, golfing holidays, long-stay and of course, the infamous Club 18-30.

With larger aircraft, more hotels and increased capacity, long haul destinations such as Mexico, the USA, Canada and Australia became more popular and provided the traveller with seemingly endless possibilities.

Ascent of Everest

Mount Everest, with the Western Cwm and Mount Everest to the left and the Lhotse Face to the right

Formerly known as 'Peak 15', surveyors discovered in 1852 that this mountain was the highest in the world at 29,002 feet (8840 metres) or 5 ½ miles (8.8 km) and they named it after their Surveyor General, George Everest. The Himalayan range is 1500 miles (2414 km) long and contains some of the world's highest peaks.

To the north of the Himalayas lies Tibet and to the south, Nepal. Before the Second World War, the only access was through Tibet. Nepal was in effect, closed to visitors.

In 1924, a British team led by Mallory and Irvine, set out as the second expedition (the first having attempted the ascent in 1922) to scale Mount Everest from the north. Mallory and Irvine disappeared on the third attempt. Mallory's body was found in 1999 at a height of 26,760 feet and although there is no evidence that he reached the summit, it is known that he achieved a new world altitude record of 28,126 feet.

It was George Mallory who provided the classic answer to the question of why someone would want to climb Mount Everest; he said "Because it is there". It was a challenge.

After the Second World War, Tibet was closed to outsiders and Nepal opened up. This provided the opportunity for an attempt to climb Everest from the south.

In 1951, Eric Shipton (who had taken part in several Everest expeditions before the war and in 1935, had met with Sherpa Tenzing Norgay) led the Everest Reconnaissance Expedition along with a young climber called Edmund Hillary. They brought back a good deal of useful information, such as weather conditions, the effects of altitude and the supplies and support that would be needed. Before that, it was not known whether men would be able to survive at those heights.

In 1952, a Swiss team attempted the climb and although they managed to reach the upper regions, they did not reach the summit.

In October 1952, Colonel John Hunt was invited by the Royal Geographical Society and the Alpine Club, to bring together a dozen of the best climbers and to equip and provision a new team for a fresh assault on the mountain.

Suitable boots had to be specially made. Light but strong nylon cotton material - suitable for withstanding 100 mile an hour winds common to Everest - was tested and used for tents and food was vacuum-packed so it was easier to pack and lighter to carry.

Kathmandu – the capital of Nepal – was the starting point for this epic journey and this was where the team met their Sherpa companions. There were no roads into Nepal and all the equipment and provisions had to be carried in or brought in by cable railway.

350 extra porters from Kathmandu helped to carry the equipment and provisions to a camp at a height of 14,000 feet. They were then paid and returned to the town.

Kathmandu itself is located at a height of 4,000 feet (1219.2 metres) and is 170 miles (274 km) from the base of Everest, which stands at 18,000 feet (5486 metres). The foothills of the 'Goddess Mother of the World' are higher than most mountains.

The rest of the group set off to climb to 18,000 feet where they established a base camp at the foot of the ice fall and dropped their thirteen tons of supplies. Three tons of provisions had to be carried to the next camp at the Western Cwm ('cwm' is the Welsh word for 'valley) (21,200 feet or 6462 metres) and then 500 pounds delivered to the next camp at the South Col (26,000 feet or 7925 metres) ready for the final attempt on the summit.

A reconnaissance party comprising Hillary, Ward and one of the expert Sherpa climbers marked out and secured the route which others would follow. The ice fall is some 2,000 feet (609 metres) high and it was estimated that it would take 3 days to get to camp 4.

A transit camp was established at 20,500 feet (6248 metres), 2,000 feet (609 metres) from the base of the ice fall and 9,000 feet (2743 metres) from the summit. The team reported that most mornings were fine but that it snowed heavily every afternoon.

At a height of 20,000 feet (6096 metres), the first serious effects of a lack of oxygen were noted and the climbers began to feel breathless and to tire easily. Every step was an effort and the pace of work slowed significantly.

Lowe and Sherpa Ang Nyima set out to mark and secure the route up the Lhotse Face but the going was slow. A task that was estimated at four days was still not complete in nine days and there was still a thousand feet to go. Expedition Leader John Hunt sent reinforcements. Time was running out.

Tom Bourdillon and Charles Evans were selected as the first assault team and John Hunt led their support party. The plan was for them to reach the south summit and carry out a reconnaissance of the South Col. If the conditions were favourable the following day, they could attempt an ascent.

Hillary and Tenzing formed the second assault team and George Lowe and Alf Gregory would be their support team. If the first team carried out a successful reconnaissance, Hillary and Tenzing – starting from a higher camp – would attempt an assault.

Bourdillon and Evans reached the south summit, some 500 feet (152 metres) from the peak of Everest and returned to tell John Hunt about the problems and difficulties of the final ridge. They had already climbed higher than any climber before them.

The next day (May 27th) was a wasted day. The weather conditions deteriorated, the winds increased and there was heavy snow. The would-be climbers were confined to their tent.

The following day the storm subsided and finally, after 11 attempts and 30 years of disappointment, two men stood on the roof of the world.

The coronation of Queen Elizabeth II

Her Majesty Queen Elizabeth II and His Royal Highness Prince Philip, Duke of Edinburgh following the Coronation in 1953.

Queen Elizabeth came to the throne at the age of 25, following the death of her father King George VI on February 6th 1952.

To allow an appropriate period of mourning for the King and to ensure sufficient time to plan the coronation, it was decided that the event would take place on June 2nd 1953.

The Queen's beloved grandmother, the formidable Queen Mary, died on March 24th 1953 but had left explicit instructions that her death should in no way delay or affect the coronation.

Queen Mary had taught the young Elizabeth about the duties and responsibilities of being a monarch. She and her husband are credited with doing much to modernise the monarchy during their reign and her husband – George V – was responsible for changing the name of the family from Saxe-Coburg and Gotha to the more British-sounding Windsor, thus founding the House of Windsor.

The Coronation Commission – chaired by Prince Philip – held its first meeting in April 1952. Other committees were convened under the chairmanship of the Duke of Norfolk who – in his role as Earl Marshall – had overall responsibility for staging the event. The set design (i.e the provision of public toilets, street decorations etc) came under the jurisdiction of David Eccles, Minister of Works. He stated that "The Earl Marshall is the Producer. I am the stage manager".

That being the case, the costume designer was the talented Norman Hartnell, a favourite of the Queen and the Queen Mother. In 1947, Hartnell had designed the wedding dress of the then Princess Elizabeth when she married Prince Philip.

He designed the exquisite white silk coronation dress embroidered with the emblems of the four home countries and of the countries of the Commonwealth and also designed the simple white linen dress to fit over the coronation gown for the anointing.

The coronation of King George VI in 1937 had been broadcast on radio and in the first major outside broadcast, the coronation procession was filmed but cameras were not allowed in Westminster Abbey.

This was the first time a full coronation was broadcast live on television but at the request of the Queen, the most sacred part of the ceremony – the anointing – was not filmed.

There had been several rehearsals, with the Duchess of Norfolk standing in for the Queen but the Queen herself attended two rehearsals at the Abbey; one on May 22nd and one on May 29th. In addition, she wore the State Crown whilst going about her daily routine at Buckingham Palace, so she could get used to its weight and how to move whilst wearing it.

Queen Elizabeth was crowned at Westminster Abbey by the Archbishop of Canterbury in front of 8,000 invited guests from all over the Commonwealth and beyond. At the moment the crown was placed upon her head, the peers of the realm replaced their own coronets, the congregation shouted "God save the Queen" and a 21-gun salute was fired from the Tower of London.

The Queen returned to the throne and the Archbishop and bishops followed by the peers – led by HRH Prince Philip, Duke of Edinburgh, Prince Henry, Duke of Gloucester and Prince Edward, Duke of Kent - all pledged allegiance to their sovereign.

The Queen took communion then the congregation recited the Lord's Prayer before the Queen and her entourage processed to the Abbey's Great West Door.

The nation celebrated with street parties and as very few people had televisions in those days, many people invited their friends, relatives and neighbours to their homes to watch the coronation live on their small black and white tv's. Copies of the film were rushed to Canada by special plane so the Canadians could watch the coronation the same day and other copies were flown to the USA and Australia.

It was estimated that worldwide, the total audience for the coronation was around 277 million. Three million watched the procession in person along the streets of London and 29,000 service personnel from all over the Commonwealth took part, with a further 15,800 lining the route.

Commemorative coins and medals were struck and acorns from the oak trees in Windsor Great Park were shipped to Commonwealth countries where they were planted in parks, public gardens and cemeteries. They became known as 'Coronation Oaks' or 'Royal Oaks'.

On Coronation Day, news reached London that Sherpa Norgay Tenzing and Edmund Hillary has successfully reached the summit of Mount Everest on May 29th

Elvis Presley – king of rock and roll.

Elvis Aaron Presley (1935-1977)

The photograph shown is a publicity still from the 1957 film 'Jailhouse Rock' in which Presley co-starred with Judy Tyler and Mickey Shaughnessy.

The film was distributed by MGM and the sequence pictured is considered by some to be Presley's greatest moment on screen.

Elvis Aaron Presley was born on January 8th 1935 in Tupelo, Mississippi to Gladys and Vernon Presley and when Elvis was 13, the family moved to Memphis. It was there that he began his music career.

In 1954, Elvis was recording with Sun Records. His band consisted of Elvis on rhythm acoustic guitar, Scotty Moore on lead guitar and Bill Black, the bass player. They were joined in 1955 by drummer, DJ Fontana.

RCA Victor acquired the contract in a deal brokered by 'Colonel' Tom Parker, who would go on to manage Presley for the next twenty years. Parker had no claim to the military title of 'colonel', having never served in the forces but it did him no harm as a courtesy title.

Parker seemed to have had a somewhat shady past. He arrived in the USA aged 18 by jumping ship. It was believed that he had committed a crime in his native Netherlands and his immigrant status was hidden for many years.

He somehow drifted into music promotion and discovered Presley.

Parker could see that Presley had talent and his voice, personality and presentation of a song were different from anything that had gone before. Parker understood how to 'market' him.

Following a series of hit records and appearances on television, Parker signed Presley up to make a series of films. His first – 'Love Me Tender' – was released in 1956.

The partnership worked well for both men and they became wealthy; Parker was taking 50% of Presley's earnings but his addiction to gambling ensured he frittered most of it away.

Presley was called up into the army in 1958 and was sent to Germany, where he met his future wife, Priscilla Beaulieu. She was only 14 when they met and their courtship lasted over seven years, part of which they were living together. Colonel Parker thought this might harm Presley's reputation so he insisted they got married. They finally did so in 1967.

When Presley returned to the US from Germany in 1960, he relaunched his career with some of his most popular and critically successful work.

Parker signed him up to make more films and even though Presley hated making films, he did as he was told but by this time, the scripts he was being offered were becoming more banal and mediocre and were not critical successes.

Parker managed most of Presley's personal life as well as his professional life but in the 1960's – when Presley's addiction to junk food and unauthorised prescription medication began to seriously affect his health – Parker left him.

An inquiry in 1980 into Parker's management practices found them to be 'unethical'.

Presley's addictions escalated and he and Priscilla divorced in 1973. His health continued to deteriorate and on August 16th 1977, the 'King of Rock and Roll' died.

The assassination of President Kennedy

President John F Kennedy and the First Lady November 22nd 1963

The presidential motorcade travelling through Dallas moments before the President was assassinated.

John Fitzgerald Kennedy was born on May 29th 1917, the second of nine children in a wealthy, Catholic family.

His father – Joseph Patrick Kennedy (aka Joe Kennedy) - had made a multi-million- dollar fortune through banking, shipbuilding, the film industry and playing the stock market. Joe established trusts for all his children, ensuring their lifelong financial independence.

John Kennedy joined the US Navy in 1941 and saw action in the South Pacific, where a Japanese destroyer sank his patrol boat. Kennedy was seriously injured but managed to lead his men to safety.

Kennedy became a high flyer in Democratic politics and served three terms in the House of Representatives (1947-1953) advocating higher wages, lower prices, better working conditions, higher Social Security benefits for older people, more social housing and lower rents. Kennedy never lost an election.

On 12th September 1953, Kennedy married wealthy socialite, Jacqueline Bouvier. They had met in 1952 when he was a Congressman.

Kennedy destroyed the widely-held belief that no Roman Catholic could become President when he won the Primary in protestant West Virginia and he reiterated his belief in the separation between church and state.

His first foray into foreign affairs as President failed spectacularly. The CIA had trained and equipped a group of anti-communist Cuban exiles and the US Joint Chiefs of Staff recommended to Kennedy that they should use this group to initiate an uprising against Castro.

Every man in the group was either killed or captured and Castro was never in any danger of being overthrown. Whilst Kennedy took 'sole responsibility', he told his father that he would never again accept a recommendation from the Joint Chiefs of Staff without challenging it first; a wise decision that ensured Kennedy managed to save the world from certain disaster during the Cuban Missile Crisis.

JFK made his brother Robert (Bobby) Kennedy the second most influential and powerful man in the country and his chief adviser, by appointing him Attorney General.

In spite of JFK's reputation as a womaniser, he was popular in the USA and abroad and the 'Kennedy Clan' always presented a united front. The family was often seen together in public and became almost as famous as the President and the First Lady.

In May 1961, Kennedy made a memorable speech in which he committed the USA to landing a man on the Moon and returning him safely to Earth before the end of the decade. He wouldn't live to see the achievement of his challenge but with only five months to spare before the deadline, Neil Armstrong, a 38 -year -old American, became the first man to set foot on the Moon.

On November 22nd 1963, the President and the First Lady were sitting in an open-top limousine in a motorcade through Dallas, Texas when shots rang out. President Kennedy was struck twice; once in the neck and once in the head. He died soon afterwards.

Lee Harvey Oswald was charged with the murder of the President but two days later – during a brief public appearance as he was being transferred to another jail – Oswald was shot and killed by Jack Ruby, a nightclub owner who had associations with the criminal underworld.

Jack Ruby was convicted of murdering Lee Harvey Oswald and was sentenced to death but later, his conviction was successfully appealed and Ruby was granted a new trial. It was when Ruby was in jail awaiting his new trial date that he died of complications of lung cancer.

The unusual circumstances of Kennedy's death, the 'convenient' shooting of Oswald before he could stand trial, and the subsequent death of Jack Ruby, raised questions.

To this day, JFK's assassination remains the subject of rumour, speculation and numerous conspiracy theories.

There is a saying that everyone who was alive then remembers where they were when they heard the news that President Kennedy had been assassinated.

Can you remember where you were?

The Beatles – the phenomenon of 'Beatlemania'

'The Beatles' appearance on the Ed Sullivan Show in 1964.

Formed in Liverpool in 1960, the band who became universally known as 'The Beatles', is regarded as the most influential, commercially successful and critically acclaimed band of all time.

It all began in March 1957, when a 16 year old John Lennon formed a skiffle group. In July of the same year, John met 15 year old Paul McCartney and invited him to join the group. The following February, Paul invited 15 year old George

Harrison into the group, though John wasn't too keen at first.

Following appearances under several different names, in August 1960, The Beatles formed and began a 3 ½ month residency in Hamburg, having been joined by drummer, Pete Best. The band was well-received in the main and the experience certainly opened the eyes of four young lads from Liverpool.

During their second residency in Hamburg, the group's bass guitarist Stuart Sutcliffe, decided he wanted to remain in the country with his new girlfriend, so Paul McCartney began playing bass.

On their return to Liverpool, the band played various clubs, most notably The Cavern, where they were spotted by Brian Epstein in November 1961. Two months later, the group appointed him as their manager for a 25% share of their earnings.

George Martin – often referred to as the 5th Beatle – signed the group to Parlophone (owned by the EMI Group) and the group's first recording session with George Martin was on June 6th 1962. Almost immediately he told the group that they needed a new drummer, so in August, Ringo Starr was brought in to replace Pete Best.

Their first successful single was 'Love Me Do', which was released in October. At another recording session in November 1963, George Martin suggested re-recording an earlier, unreleased version of 'Please, Please Me' and after the session, he told the boys "You've just made your first number 1"...and he was right.

Between 1963 and 1970, 11 of the 12 albums released by The Beatles reached number 1 in the UK. In April 1963, the group's second hit 'From Me to You' was released and was the first of a string of hits. Seventeen of the 18 singles they released between 1963 and 1969 reached number 1. The single 'She Loves You' – released in August 1964 – became the first single to sell a million copies.

Lennon and McCartney formed a successful song-writing partnership. As well as writing many of The Beatles' songs, they also wrote 'Goodbye' for Mary Hopkin, Love of the Loved', Step Inside, Love' and 'It's for You' for Cilla Black, 'World Without Love' and 'Nobody I Know' for Peter and Gordon and 'Bad to Me' and 'I'll Keep You Satisfied' for Billy J Kramer and the Dakotas.

The group brought about a phenomenon known as 'Beatlemania', where hysterical fans would 'mob' the group, screaming, sobbing uncontrollably and often fainting. In the case of a concert at Plymouth, police were forced to use high pressure water hoses to try and control the hysterical crowd.

When the group launched in America, an estimated 73 million people – the largest audience ever for an American tv programme at that time - watched their appearance on the Ed Sullivan Show in 1964. A few days later, they made another appearance on the Ed Sullivan show, watched this time by around 70 million viewers.

They played live at the famous Shea Stadium in August 1965 to an audience of 55,600, although the group complained that the fans screamed so loudly that they could neither hear themselves or each other and had to watch each other's mouths to follow a song. Unfortunately, the sound system wasn't up to the job of a music concert. It was only used for broadcasting on a baseball or American football game.

Other critically acclaimed albums followed and showed the group being more experimental. They included 'Revolver',

'Sgt Pepper', 'Magical Mystery Tour', 'Let it Be', 'The White Album' and 'Rubber Soul'.

The band had given up touring and concentrated on developing their music, although they had two well-received films in quick succession; the black-and-white 'A Hard Day's Night' followed by the colour film 'Help!'. Later came 'Yellow Submarine' and 'Magical Mystery Tour'.

Following the death of Brian Epstein in 1967, tensions began to surface in the group and their final live performance was in 1969 on the roof of the Apple Corps building where they sang 'Get Back'.

On December 31st 1970, Paul McCartney filed for the dissolution of The Beatles partnership but it took four years before it was finally wound up.

The end of a unique, tumultuous and unequalled era which has left a lasting musical legacy.

(In 2016, Director Ron Howard released his film 'Eight Days a Week', charting The Beatles touring years and the Shea Stadium concert was included. Using digital technology, Howard and his team 'cleaned up' the original soundtrack, turned down the screaming and turned up the music. It showed that although the members of the group couldn't hear each other, the music and the vocal performances were completely 'in sync'.

Paul McCartney said it was the first time he had heard how they sounded that night).

The life and death of Martin Luther King.

Rev Martin Luther King (1929-1968)

Born Michael Luther King on January 15th 1929 in Atlanta, Georgia, King later decided to change his first name.

King's grandfather and father were Pastors of the Ebenezer Baptist Church in Atlanta and between 1960 and 1968, King joined his father as co-pastor.

He had attended segregated public schools* and gained a BA degree from Morehouse College in 1948, followed later by a BD. He enrolled in Boston University from where he received his Doctorate in 1955.

Always a tireless campaigner for civil rights, he became a member of the NAACP (National Association for the Advancement of Colored People).

King travelled more than 6 million miles and gave more than 25,000 speeches and presentations. He directed the peaceful civil rights march of 250,000 people on Washington DC in 1963 and gave his famous "I have a dream" speech from the Lincoln Memorial. He stated that it was his belief that all inhabitants of the United States would be judged by their personal qualities rather than the colour of their skin.

The "I have a dream" speech is still owned by the King family, the rights to it having been established by Rev King a month after the speech was delivered.

King was voted 'Man of the Year' by Time magazine in 1963.

In 1964, President Johnson had a law passed prohibiting racial discrimination.

Married with two sons and two daughters, King became the youngest recipient of the Nobel Peace Prize at the age of 35. He made his acceptance speech in the auditorium of the University of Oslo on August 10th 1964 and pledged to donate the $54,000 dollar prize money to the civil rights movement.

King had powerful opposition to his cause. The maverick head of the FBI – J Edgar Hoover – put King under surveillance because he suspected him of being a Communist and when King spoke against the government's policy in Vietnam, he alienated the President.

On April 4th 1968, Rev Martin Luther King was assassinated on his second-floor balcony at the Lorraine Hotel in Memphis, Tennessee by felon, fugitive and white racist James Earl Ray but whether Ray was acting alone or was part of a conspiracy, has never been established and is still the subject of debate.

"Darkness cannot drive out darkness; only light can do that. Hatred cannot drive out hatred; only love can do that"

"Injustice anywhere is a threat to justice everywhere."

('public schools' has a different meaning in the US and the UK. In the United States 'public schools' are in fact 'state schools' providing free education and are part of the state system. In the UK, the term 'public schools' actually refers to 'private schools' i.e. fee-paying establishments which are not part of the state-run, free education system.)*

Earthrise – from the Earth to the Moon

'Earthrise'

'Earthrise' – one of the most famous and recognisable images of all time - is the name given to a photograph of the Earth as seen from lunar orbit. The image was taken on December 24th 1968 by William (Bill) Anders, Lunar Module Pilot on Apollo 8.

His fellow crew members were Mission Commander Frank Borman and Command Module Pilot, James (Jim) Lovell and this was the first manned mission to orbit the Moon in preparation for a lunar landing the following year.

The back-up crew for Apollo 8 consisted of Neil Armstrong (Commander), Edwin (Buzz) Aldrin (Command Module Pilot) and Fred Haise (Lunar Module Pilot).

The following year, Armstrong and Aldrin would be the first men to walk on the Moon and in 1970, Fred Haise would take part in the 'successful failure' that was Apollo 13, where he was the Lunar Module Pilot.

In the early afternoon of December 23rd 1968, Apollo 8 was captured by the Moon's gravity and soon afterwards, the crew became the first humans to see the 'far side' of the Moon. Just before communications with NASA were lost, Jim Lovell said "We'll see you on the other side."

To the flight controllers on the ground in Mission Control, it seemed like an eternity before the signal was re-acquired and communications were restored.

The crew of Apollo 8 had joined the ranks of explorers such as Amundsen, Columbus and Drake, seeing a new land for the first time and they eagerly described to the controllers back on Earth, what they were seeing.

Before taking the colour image, Anders had first taken a black and white photo. He realised the potential of showing the blue marble of Earth set against the infinite blackness of space and asked Lovell for a colour film.

Anders took the first colour photograph followed by Lovell then Anders took another. Lovell helpfully recorded the setting as 1/250th of a second at $f/11$.

On the 9th orbit of the Moon, Bill Anders voice came over the radio, reading a short passage from the Book of Genesis:

"In the beginning, God created the heaven and the earth.
And the earth was without form, and void, and darkness was on the face of the deep
And God said 'Let there be light, and there was light...."

It was Christmas Eve.

Early on Christmas morning after completing its 10th lunar orbit, Apollo 8 left the Moon's gravity and headed home to the beautiful blue marble that they had captured so perfectly.

(In 'Life' magazine's '100 Photographs That Changed the World', wilderness photographer Galen Rowell called 'Earthrise' "The most influential environmental photograph ever taken" and it was credited by others as the beginning of the environmental movement.

On the 50th anniversary of the Apollo 8 mission, Bill Anders said "We set out to explore the Moon and discovered the Earth").

The invention of the computer - The Age of Technology.

The Osborne Computer, 1982.

It might be surprising to learn that it was a well-educated, 19th century young woman who devised the world's first computer program, especially when there were no computers in the 1800's. However, Ada Lovelace – the daughter of Lord Byron – was highly skilled in mathematics and science.

She had been impressed by the work of Charles Babbage, who referred to her as the "enchantress of numbers".

Charles Babbage (1791-1871) was an English mathematician, mechanical engineer and inventor. He invented a hand-cranked, mechanical machine consisting of 25,000 parts and weighing 15 tons, which could solve a number of mathematical calculations. Unfortunately, he did not finish building it. He began a second machine which could give mathematical results up to 13 digits. Again, it was incomplete.

Babbage's third attempt produced what he called an 'analytical engine', which could be programmed with punch cards (much like early modern computers). This enabled a program to be used repeatedly rather than having to input the data manually time and time again. It could also use the results of past data to help with future calculations.

Babbage is known as the 'father of the computer'.

Although Babbage designed the 'analytical engine', it was never built. If it had been, it would have been what we now refer to as 'Turing Complete', as are modern computers.

Named after the mathematical genius and code-breaker Alan Turing, 'Turing Complete' means that a computer can work out the result of any calculation and do what it was designed to do as well as what more complex machines can do (memory size permitting).

Ada Lovelace took an interest in Babbage's work and building on the work of an Italian mathematician, she devised the world's first computer program which would have run successfully on Babbage's Analytical Engine. Ada also worked out that in the future, computers (as they would be named much later) could probably be used for purposes other than number-crunching, such as music.

The US military uses a programming language named 'ADA', after Miss Lovelace and her image can be found on the Microsoft product authenticity hologram.

Alan Turing (1912-1954) was a highly successful pioneer of computer science – many say he invented it – and he developed the 'Turing Test' of computer intelligence. He also became known as the 'father of Artificial Intelligence' and developed the 'Turing Machine', an early general- purpose computer.

Alan Turing once said "Sometimes it is the people that no-one imagines anything of who do the things no-one can imagine."

Special computers had to be designed to accommodate the unique requirements of the space programme in the 1960's. Those familiar with the control rooms will remember the banks of computers as well as the individual ones used by the flight controllers. The modern iPhone has 100,000 times more processing power than the computer which landed men on the Moon in 1969.

In the years following the Apollo missions, progress on the development of computers, computer systems and software was rapid.

Tim Berners-Lee (Sir Timothy Berners-Lee, born 1955 in London) invented the World Wide Web in 1989 with the aim of promoting global information-sharing. He said "The original idea of the web was that it should be a collaborative space where you can communicate through sharing information."

He wrote the first web client and server in 1990 and refined the specifications on URL's, HTML and HTTP. It is also possible that he recognised that the web could be used for other purposes. He said "You affect the world by what you browse."

Steve Jobs (1955-2011) was Chairman, Chief Executive and co-founder of Apple Computers, a company which is generally considered to lead the way in dictating the evolution of modern technology and whose brands include the iPhone, iPad and iPod.

Steve Jobs is quoted as saying "Design is not just what it looks like and feels like. Design is how it works."

Another name synonymous with computer technology is Bill Gates (born 1955) co-founder of software giant, the Microsoft Corporation and also its Chief Software Architect, President, Chairman and Chief Executive.

Microsoft was the pioneer of the microcomputer revolution and is the world's largest software company.

Mark Zuckerberg (born 1984) took computers a stage further when he co-founded then became Chairman and Chief Executive of Facebook. The aim of Facebook is simply to bring the world closer together

Computers are now in use in almost every aspect of modern life, from communications to medicine, from photography and music to animation, sport and films, aviation to space exploration and every day, new uses are being explored.

(Facebook has (as of the second quarter of 2020) 2.7 billion monthly users and 1.73 billion users accessing Facebook every day. Mark Zuckerberg himself has 116,900,318 followers of his own Facebook page).

Nelson Mandela – Fight for Freedom.

Nelson Mandela (1918-2013)

(Photograph taken at Independence Hall, Philadelphia, PA on July 4th 1993).

Rolihlahla 'Nelson' Mandela was born on 18th July 1918 in South Africa.

He studied law at Fort Hare and the University of Witwatersrand and later practised in Johannesburg.

In 1943, he joined the African National Congress. The ruling party's 'whites only' government had established a system of racial segregation in the country, known as 'apartheid' and the ANC was committed to its overthrow.

Mandela was repeatedly arrested and accused of sedition and was unsuccessfully prosecuted for treason in 1956.

Initially committed to peaceful protest, he later co-founded the more militant 'Umkhonto we Sizwe' in 1961.

Arrested and charged with conspiracy to overthrow the State, Mandela was imprisoned for life in 1962. He served 27 years between three separate institutions, the best known being at Robben Island, where he served his longest term, 1964-1982. It was a place notorious for its cruel treatment of mainly black prisoners by white prison warders.

Mandela – and most of the other prisoners – were tasked to break rocks by day, although he was eventually reassigned to work in the lime quarry. This – plus the hours he spent in a damp cell measuring 7 feet by 8 feet (2.1 metres by 2.4 metres)– probably contributed to his lung problems later in life.

At night however, Mandela worked to attain his Bachelor of Law degree from the University of London through a correspondence course, although papers and newspapers were banned so he was often placed in solitary confinement as a punishment.

Mandela studied Africaans to help him communicate with the prison warders and whilst attending Christian services, he also learnt about the Islamic faith, though Mandela was never particularly religious.

By 1990, Mandela was in the Victor Verster Prison, recovering from Tuberculosis. He was housed in warders' accommodation and finally able to have visitors and correspond with the outside world.

Meanwhile, South Africa had acquired a new President in F W de Clerk, who finally realised that apartheid was unsustainable and that there was increasing pressure from outside the country as well as inside. The President released some ANC prisoners and eventually persuaded his cabinet colleagues to debate and consider legalising the previously banned ANC and freeing Mandela.

Mandela was finally freed on February 11th 1990.

In 1994, Nelson Mandela became President of a multi-national South Africa, the first black head of state elected in the first fully representative democratic elections. His government focused on dismantling the remains of the apartheid system, tackling institutional racism and promoting reconciliation. His Presidency lasted until 1999.

Said to be charismatic, well-mannered, polite and courteous, well-dressed and with a sense of humour, Mandela was also a much more complex character in private. He had embraced Communism and turned from a stance of peaceful protest to a more confrontational and aggressive style. He was said to be a womaniser when he was younger and he was married three times.

Even so, considered as the 'father of the nation' in South Africa, Mandela became an A list celebrity on the world stage, visiting and being entertained by heads of state and political leaders.

He received over 250 awards, honorary degrees and other honours, most notably the Nobel Peace Prize but also including the US Presidential Medal of Freedom and the Freedom of the City of Johannesburg. Libya awarded him the Al-Gaddafi International Award for Human Rights and Queen Elizabeth II appointed him as a Bailiff Grand Cross of the Order of St John. He also became the first living person to be made an honorary Canadian citizen.

(In 2009, the UN General Assembly declared July 18th (Mandela's birthday) 'Mandela Day' and called on people to give 67 minutes of their time to help others. This represented the 67 years Mandela devoted to the anti-apartheid movement.

Nelson Mandela died on December 5th 2013.

In 2015, the United Nations General Assembly named the amended 'Standard Minimum Rules for the Treatment of Prisoners' the 'Mandela Rules' in his honour).

Acknowledgements.

1901: The photograph of Queen Victoria was taken in 1882 by Alexander Bassano and is in the Public Domain, as the author died in 1913.

1908: Photograph of Orville and Wilbur Wright. Photographer unattributed. Public Domain work US – copyright expired. (PD-45).

1909: Photo of HMS 'Endurance' taken by Frank Hurley (1885-1962). Source: State Library of New South Wales. Catalogue record 823 227. Public Domain photo. Copyright term expired.

1911: Roald Amundsen and his team at the South Pole. This photograph is in the Public Domain. Author: Olav Bjaarland (1873-1961). Source: Project Gutenberg Literary Archive. Permission: Project Gutenberg Public Domain.

1912: Photograph of RMS 'Titanic' taken on 10th April 1912 by F G O Stuart. This work is in the Public Domain.

1914: World War 1 recruitment poster, designed by Alfred Leete. Public Domain work created by the UK Government. HMSO has declared that the expiry of Crown Copyright applies worldwide.

1922: The golden mask of Tutankhamun. Author: en:UserMykReeve. Source: Wikimedia Commons. Published under the Creative Commons Attribution Share-Alike 3.0 Unported License.

1934: This photograph of Duke and Duchess of Windsor was created in Italy in 1934 and is in the Public Domain. The author was widely acknowledged to be Vincenzo Lavioso but this has been challenged. It is now thought to be the work of Angelo Lavioso, as the photo bears his signature.

1939: World War 2 poster. Artist unknown. Produced by the Ministry of Information, UK Government. HMSO has declared that the expiry of Crown Copyright applies worldwide.

1948: Source: National Health Service, Western Isles Health Board. NHS Leaflet was created by the UK Government and is in the Public Domain. HMSO has declared that the expiry of Crown Copyright applies worldwide.

1953: Photograph of Mount Everest. Source: Moving Mountains Trust. Reprinted under the Creative Commons Attribution 2.0 Generic License.

1953: Photograph of HM Queen Elizabeth II and HRH Prince Philip taken on June 2nd 1953 by Cecil Beaton. This is a Public Domain work created by the UK Government. HMSO has declared that the expiry of Crown Copyright applies worldwide.

1957: Publicity still of Elvis Presley from the film 'Jailhouse Rock'. Public Domain work. The US Library of Congress found no copyright in existence in December 2000.

1963: Photograph of President JF Kennedy and Jackie Kennedy taken on November 11th 1963 by Victor Hugo King. The photo was released into the Public Domain.

1964: The Beatles appearance on the Ed Sullivan Show. This image has been declared to be in the Public Domain by the copyright owner OR the copyright has expired.

1968: Photograph of the Earth from the Moon (Earthrise) taken by Apollo 8 astronaut Bill Anders on December 24th 1968. NASA image AS 08-14- 2383. Public Domain work.

1968 - Photograph of Martin Luther King Jnr taken on April 4th 1968. A photograph of Swedish origin created before 1970 and therefore in the Public Domain. The United States Domain tag – PD Sweden (i.e. photographic images in the Public Domain and of Swedish origin, taken before 1969).

1982: Osborne Computer. Produced by Casey Feser and reproduced under the Creative Commons Attribution 2.0 Generic License.

1993: The photograph of Nelson Mandela was taken on 4th July 1993 at Independence Hall, Philadelphia, Pennsylvania. This is a work of the US Federal Government and is in the Public Domain. Source: from the Public Papers of the Presidents of the United States. (National Archives Identifier Number: 2569290).

Cover Image: Cover image of the Messier 5 globular cluster was created by NASA/ESA and Hubble Space and is in the public domain.

Sources:

Documentary film 'Conquest of Everest'. Released December 7th 1953. Produced by Countryman Films. Distributed by British Lion Film Corporation.

'The Ascent of Everest' by John Hunt. Published by Hodder and Stoughton 1993 (first published in Britain in 1953).

Television documentary 'Spying on the Royals'. Channel 4 documentary first shown in 2017.

'That Woman, the life of Wallis Simpson, Duchess of Windsor' by Anne Sebba. Published by Phoenix in 2012.

Nursing Times, January 8th 2008.

Explorations: Great moments of discovery from the Royal Geographical Society. Published in the UK by Scriptum Editions, 1997.

The Nobel Prize Website. Published by the Norwegian Nobel Institute.

'The Golden Age of Travel – the romantic years of tourism in images from the Thomas Cook archives' by Andrew Williamson. Published by Thomas Cook Publishing, 1998.

'The Discovery of the Tomb of Tutankhamun' by Howard Carter and Arthur C Mace. Published by Dover Publications Inc., 1977.

Wikipedia and Wikimedia.

'Failure is Not an Option' by Gene Kranz, former flight director at NASA. Published by Berkley Publications in 2000.

'Titanic – an illustrated history' by Don Lynch, illustrated by Ken Marschall. Published by Hodder and Stoughton, 1992.

By the same author:

"I Know That One!"   quiz book.

"I Know That One, Too!"   quiz book.

'A Passport Full of Stamps'

'Another Passport Full of Stamps'

'A Journey Through Time – travels in Egypt' volume 1

'An Egypt Itinerary'…. (e-book only)

'Behind the Myths – Introduction to Ancient Egypt'

'Behind Closed Doors – Daily Life in Ancient Egypt'

'Twenty in Twenty More'

Coming soon:

'A Journey Through Time… travels in Egypt' volume 2.

'The Mouse and the Moon Men – travels in Florida'

Facebook page: Books By Ally

Email: booksbyally@outlook.com

Printed in Great Britain
by Amazon